CW01218780

Crazy Big Trucks

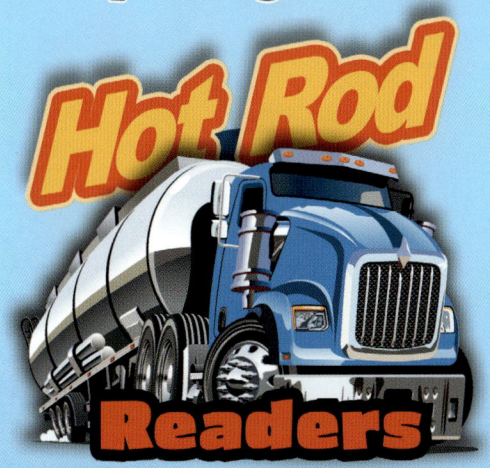

Hot Rod Readers

Craig A. Lopetz

TABLE OF CONTENTS

What Are Crazy Big Trucks?	2
Glossary	23
Index	23

A Crabtree Seedlings Book

CRABTREE
Publishing Company
www.crabtreebooks.com

What Are Crazy Big Trucks?

Crazy big trucks are **artist** drawings.

Some are made with **airbrush** paints.

Others are drawn on a computer.

Some crazy big trucks **haul** logs.

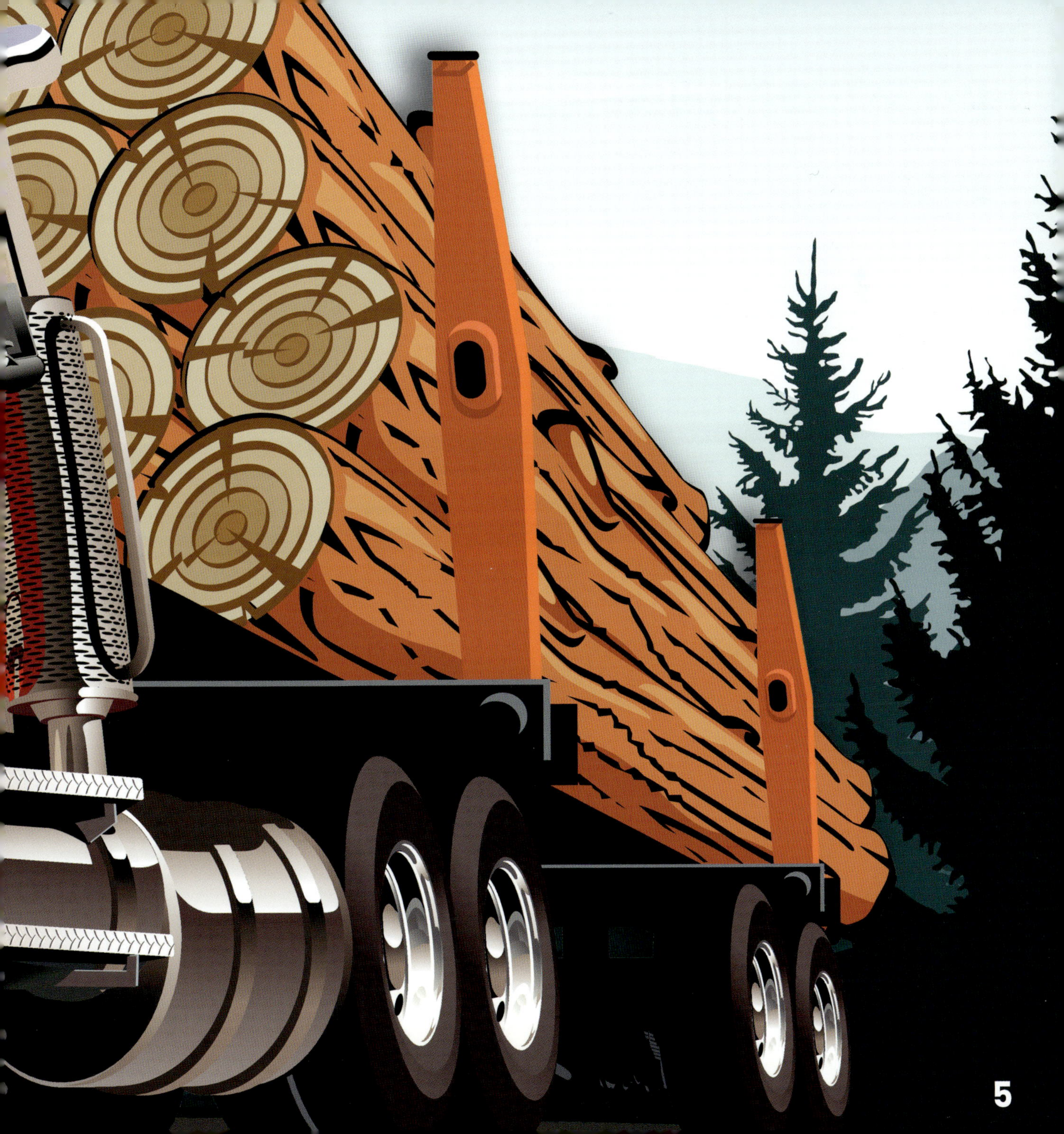

Some haul gas for our cars.

7

Some crazy big trucks carry crazy cars.

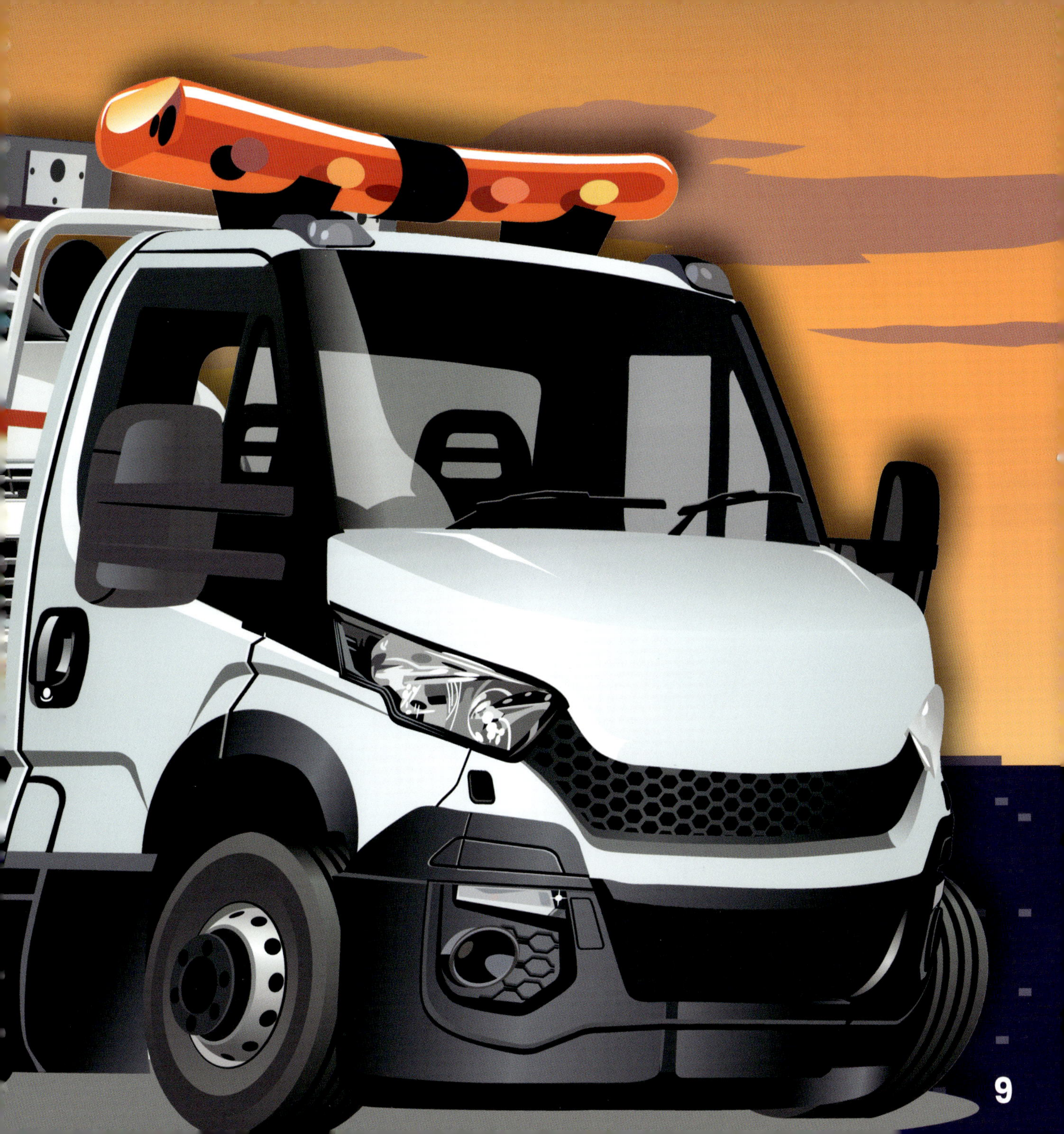

Crazy big trucks take our trash.

11

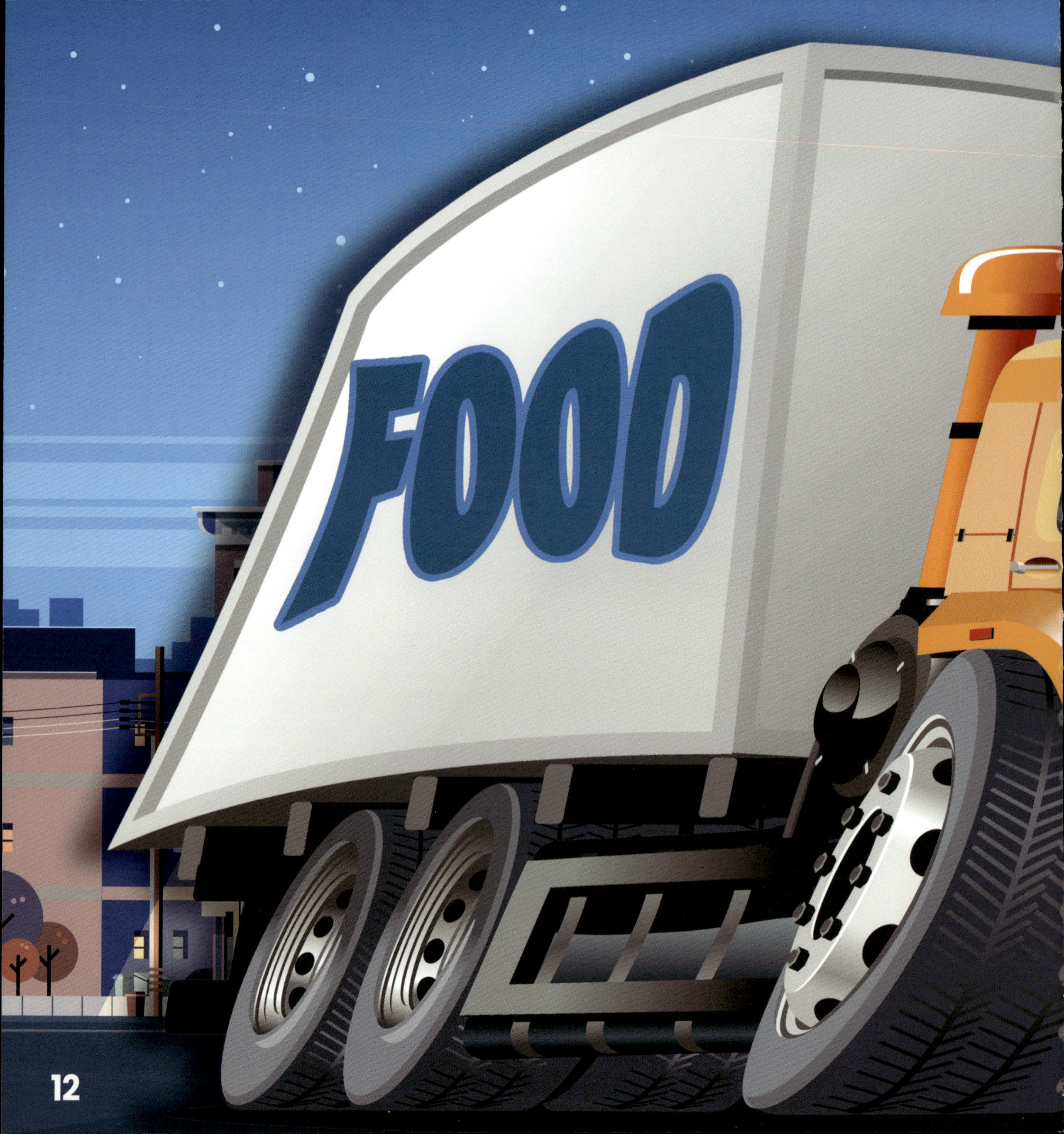
FOOD

Crazy big trucks bring food to our stores.

14

There are crazy big fire trucks.

And crazy big trucks that **tow** other big trucks.

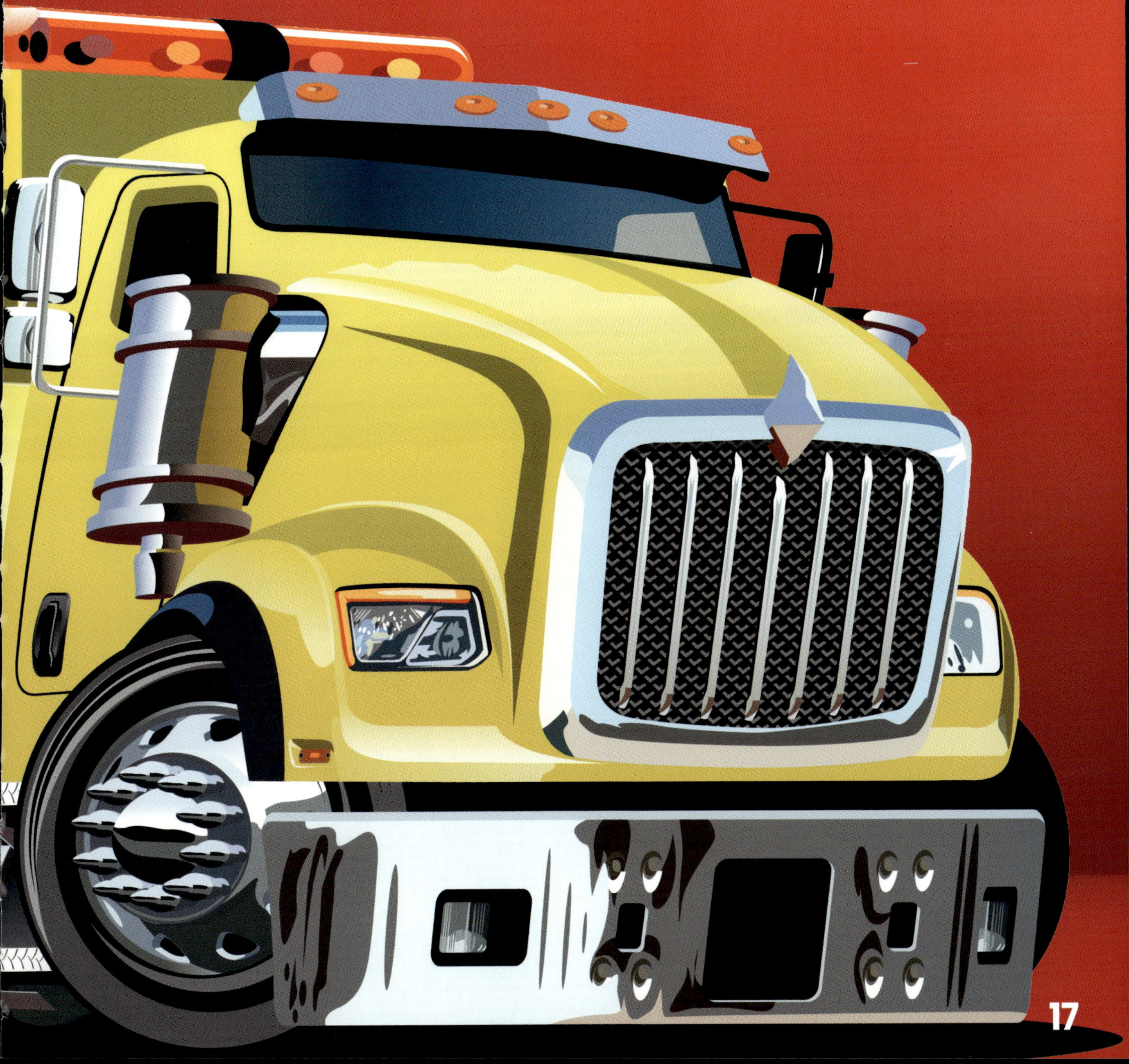

Some crazy big trucks pick things up.

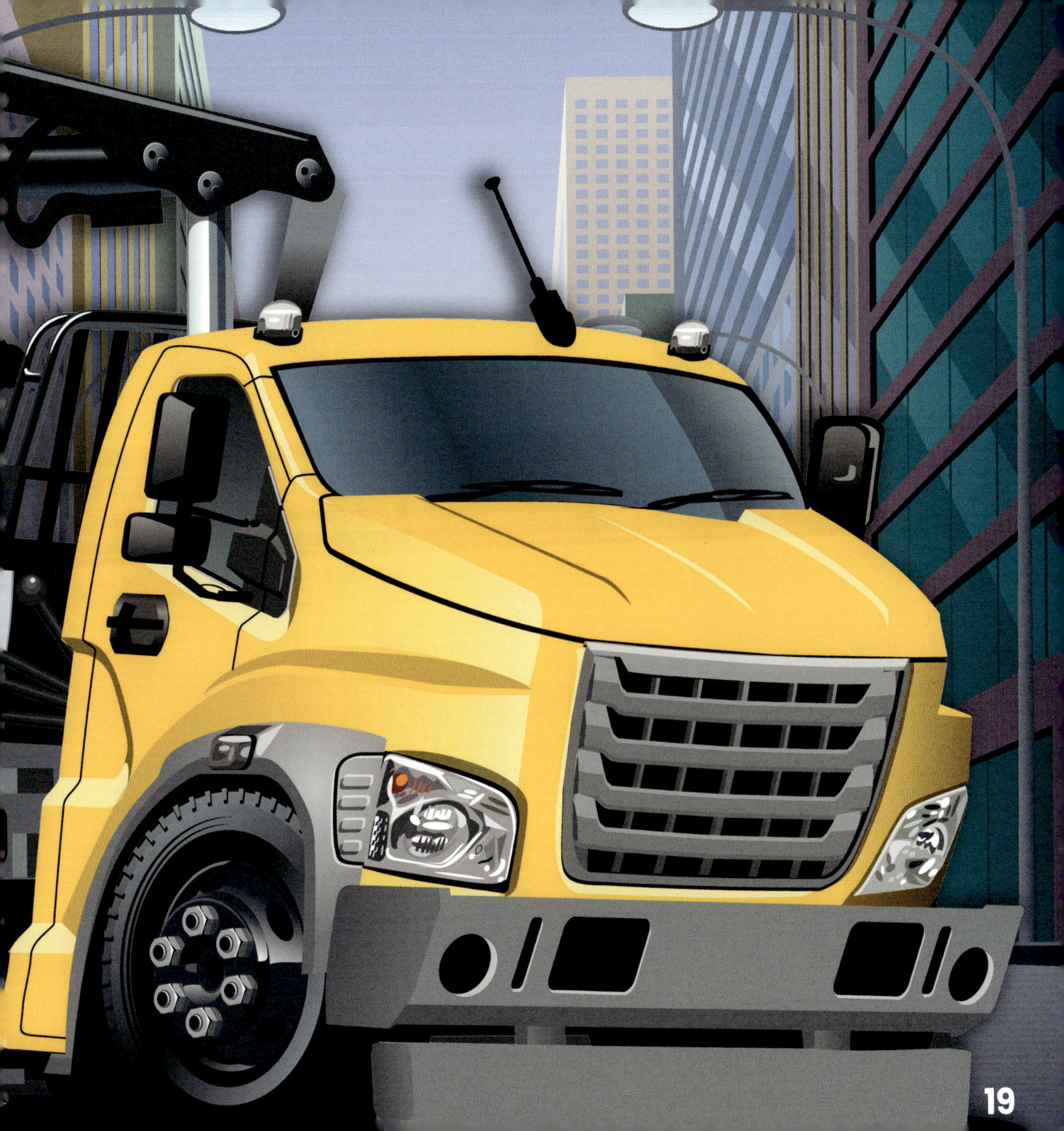

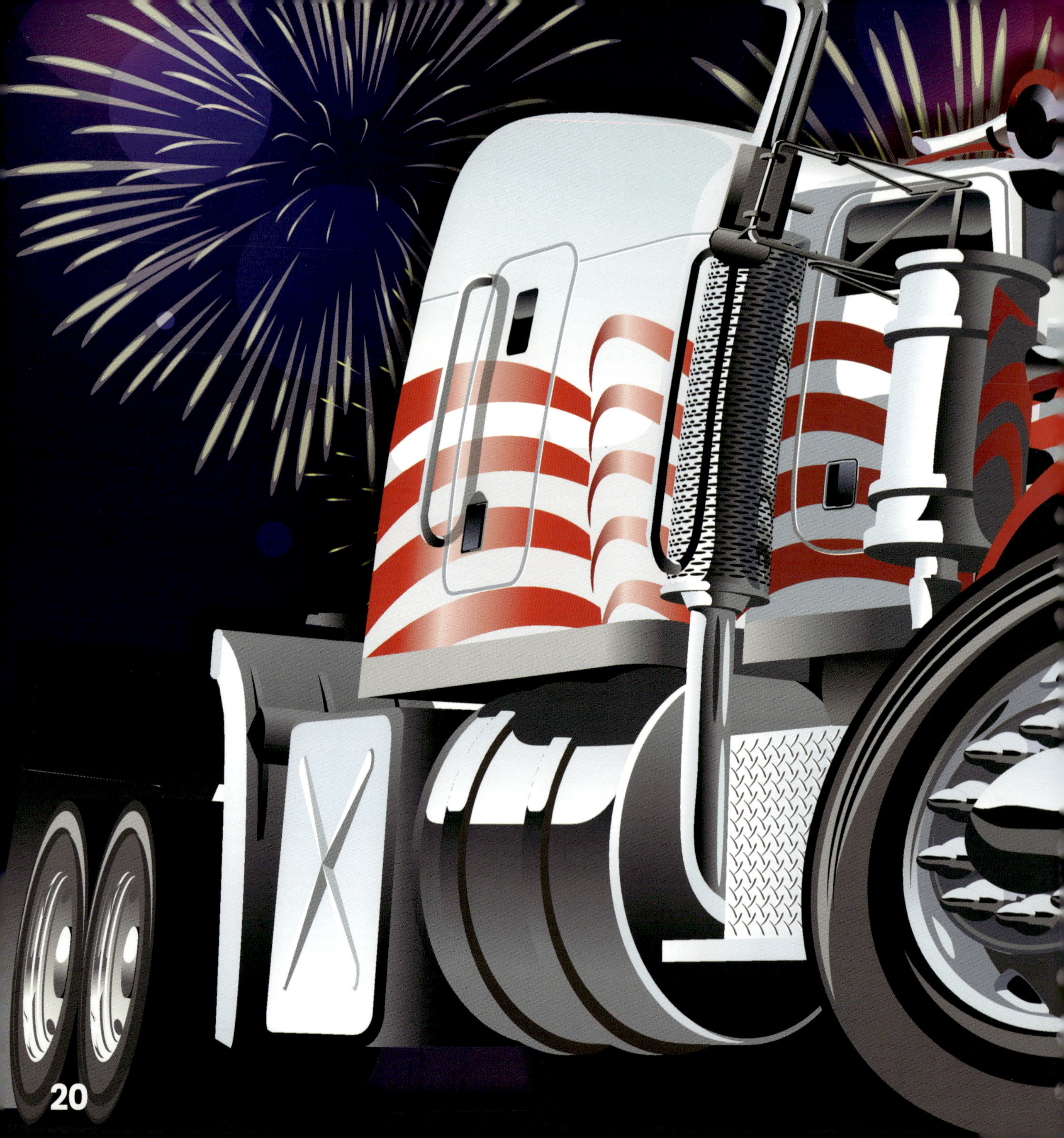

Crazy big trucks can be red, white, and blue.

Real Big Trucks and Crazy Big Trucks

Red, White, and Blue Tractor

Log Hauler

Garbage Truck

22

Glossary

airbrush (AIR-brush): An airbrush is a tool that sprays paint.

artist (AR-tist): An artist is someone who is very good at drawing, painting, or making things.

haul (HAWL): To haul is to transport something with a vehicle.

tow (TOH): To tow is to pull something behind you with a rope or chain.

Index

crazy cars   8
fire truck   15
garbage truck   10, 22
log hauler   4, 22
tow   16

School-to-Home Support for Caregivers and Teachers

This book helps children grow by letting them practice reading. Here are a few guiding questions to help the reader build his or her comprehension skills. Possible answers appear here in red.

Before Reading

- **What do I think this book is about?** I think this book is about very big trucks on the highways. I think this book is about crazy trucks on the roads.

- **What do I want to learn about this topic?** I want to learn more about different kinds of trucks. I want to learn what a person has to do to become a truck driver.

During Reading

- **I wonder why...** I wonder why some trucks can carry crazy cars. I wonder why there aren't any firefighters putting the fire out.

- **What have I learned so far?** I have learned that big trucks are used to bring food to the grocery store. I have learned that a big tow truck is needed to tow other big trucks.

After Reading

- **What details did I learn about this topic?** I have learned that big trucks are needed to bring things from one place to another place. I have learned that trucks can be painted bright colors.

- **Read the book again and look for the glossary words.** I see the word *airbrush* on page 2, and the word *haul* on page 4. The other glossary words are found on page 23.

Library and Archives Canada Cataloguing in Publication

CIP available at Library and Archives Canada

Library of Congress Cataloging-in-Publication Data

CIP available at Library of Congress

Crabtree Publishing Company
www.crabtreebooks.com   1–800–387–7650

Written by: Craig A. Lopetz
Print coordinator: Katherine Berti

Print book version produced jointly with Blue Door Education in 2023

Printed in the U.S.A./072022/CG20220201

Content produced and published by Blue Door Education, Melbourne Beach FL USA. This title Copyright Blue Door Education. All rights reserved. No part of this book may be reproduced or utilized in any form or by any means, electronic or mechanical including photocopying, recording, or by any information storage and retrieval system without permission in writing from the publisher.

PHOTO CREDITS:
www.shutterstock.com, www.istock.com. Cover images: istock.com | mechanick. Pages 2-3: shutterstock.com | Mechanik, istock.com | humonia, istock.com | scyther5. Pages 4-5: istock.com | Mechanic, istock.com | Katerina Sisperova. Pages 6-7: istock.com | Mechanic, shutterstock.com | Doremi. Pages 8-9: istock.com | Mechanic, shutterstock.com | Arunna. Pages 10-11: istock.com | Mechanic, shutterstock.com | ProStockStudio. Pages 12-13: istock.com | Mechanic, shutterstock.com | ProStockStudio. Pages 14-15: istock.com | Mechanic, shutterstock.com | ProStockStudio. Pages 16-17: istock.com | Mechanic, shutterstock.com | weedezign. Pages 18-19: istock.com | Mechanic, istock.com | Malchev. Pages 20-21: istock.com | Mechanic, shutterstock.com | milezaway. Pages 22-23: istock.com | Darinburt, RWB

Published in the United States
Crabtree Publishing
347 Fifth Ave.
Suite 1402-145
New York, NY 10016

Published in Canada
Crabtree Publishing
616 Welland Ave.
St. Catharines, Ontario
L2M 5V6